Contents

Cool New Costumes! 2

Who is Who? 10

Look For 11

Cool New Costumes! 12

The Coolest Costume 16

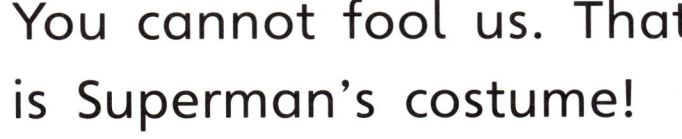

Who is Who?

Look For ...

Can you spot eight seashells?

The Coolest Costume

Who has the coolest costume?

If you had a super-costume, what would it look like?